AF594699

U.S. Government Q&A!

Who Can Run for PRESIDENT?

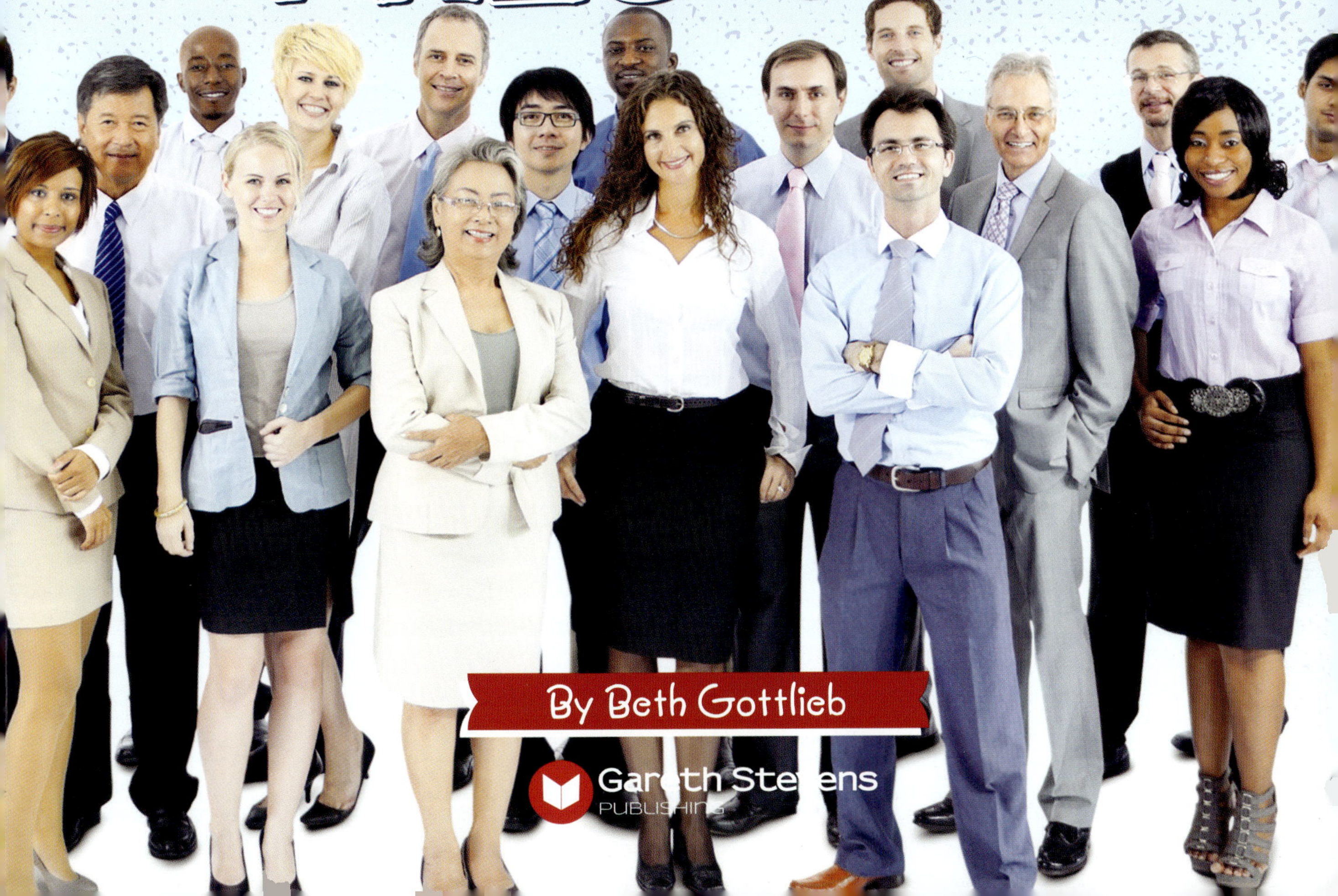

By Beth Gottlieb

Please visit our website, www.garethstevens.com. For a free color catalog of all our high-quality books, call toll free 1-800-542-2595 or fax 1-877-542-2596.

Library of Congress Cataloging-in-Publication Data
Names: Gottlieb, Beth, author.
Title: Who can run for president? / Beth Gottlieb.
Description: Buffalo, New York : Gareth Stevens Publishing, 2026. | Series: U.S. government Q & A! | Includes index. | Audience: Grades 2-3
Identifiers: LCCN 2024046983 (print) | LCCN 2024046984 (ebook) | ISBN 9781482470178 (library binding) | ISBN 9781482470161 (paperback) | ISBN 9781482470185 (ebook)
Subjects: LCSH: Presidents–United States–Juvenile literature. | Presidential candidates–United States–Juvenile literature.
Classification: LCC JK517 .G68 2026 (print) | LCC JK517 (ebook) | DDC 352.230973–dc23/eng/20241107
LC record available at https://lccn.loc.gov/2024046983
LC ebook record available at https://lccn.loc.gov/2024046984

First Edition

Published in 2026 by
Gareth Stevens Publishing
2544 Clinton Street
Buffalo, NY 14224

Copyright © 2026 Gareth Stevens Publishing

Designer: Andrea Davison-Bartolotta
Editor: Kristen Nelson

Photo credits: Cover, p. 1 Rawpixel.com/Shutterstock.com; series art (paper, feather) Incomible/Shutterstock.com; series art (blue banner, red banner, stars) pingbat/Shutterstock.com; p. 4 Gorodenkoff/Shutterstock.com; p. 5 Joseph Sohm/Shutterstock.com; p. 7 (Obama, Biden, Bush, Trump) courtesy of Library of Congress; p. 7 (Clinton, H. W. Bush) courtesy of the National Archives; p. 9 Gino Santa Maria/Shutterstock.com; p. 11 Rebekah Zemansky/Shutterstock.com; p. 13 mark reinstein/Shutterstock.com; pp. 14, 15 (top) Philip Yabut/Shutterstock.com; p. 15 (bottom) ClaudsintheClouds/Shutterstock.com; p. 16 Nerthuz/Shutterstock.com; p. 17 Artos/Shutterstock.com; p. 18Vic Hinterlang/Shutterstock.com; p. 19 Sage Ross/Flickr.com; p. 21 Alan Mazzocco/Shutterstock.com.

All rights reserved. No part of this book may be reproduced in any form without permission in writing from the publisher, except by a reviewer.

Printed in the United States of America

Some of the images in this book illustrate individuals who are models. The depictions do not imply actual situations or events.

CPSIA compliance information: Batch #CSGS26: For further information contact Gareth Stevens, New York, New York at 1-800-542-2595.

Contents

Words in the glossary appear in **bold** type the first time they are used in the text.

America Votes

United States citizens vote to choose their leaders. This includes the U.S. president. The president leads the executive branch of the government, which carries out laws. The president serves as commander in chief of the armed forces. They are the face of the United States to the rest of the world too.

Being president is a big job. Because of this, the American people often think carefully about who they are voting for. But first, they must see who will step up to run for president!

George W. Bush ran for president—and won—in 2000 and 2004. His father, George H. W. Bush, was president from 1989 to 1993. However, you don't have to have a family member in **politics** to run for president!

How Old Are You?

The U.S. Constitution lays out the basic laws of the United States. It lists just three requirements for those serving as the U.S. president. The first has to do with age: The president must be at least 35 years old.

Most presidents have been in their 50s when **elected**. Donald Trump is the oldest person to become president. He was 78 when elected for the second time in 2024. John F. Kennedy was the youngest person elected president. He was just 43 years old in 1960.

Government Guides

Supreme Court justice Joseph Story wrote that it made sense that the Constitution would have an age requirement "considering the nature of the duties ... and the solid wisdom and **experience**" needed to be president.

Recent Presidential Ages

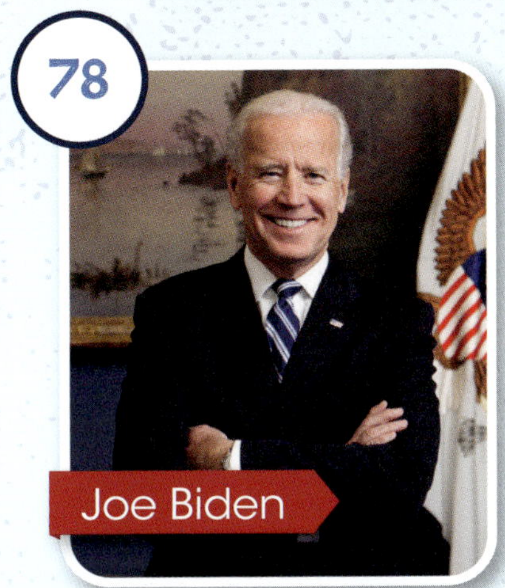

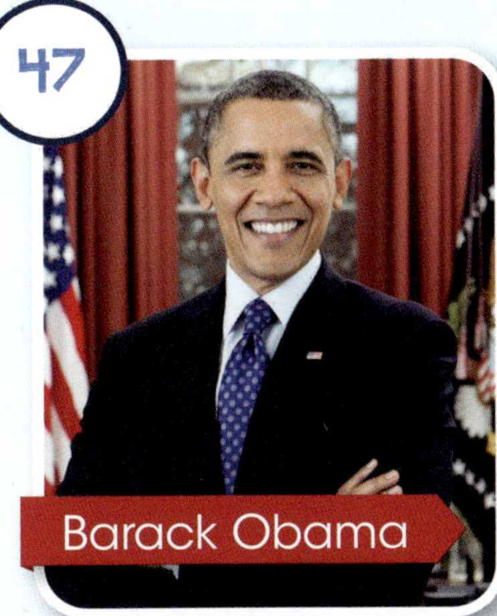

○ = age when first took office

The first U.S. president, George Washington, was 57 years old when he first took office. Over the past 35 years, presidents have ranged in age from 46 to 78!

Born in the USA

The Constitution says a person must be born a U.S. citizen to become president. The writers of the Constitution likely included this requirement because they wanted a person to be loyal only to the United States.

The Constitution requires U.S. presidents to have lived in the United States for at least 14 years too. This allows a person to take part in the workings of the country. It also allows the American people to know someone's values and ideas.

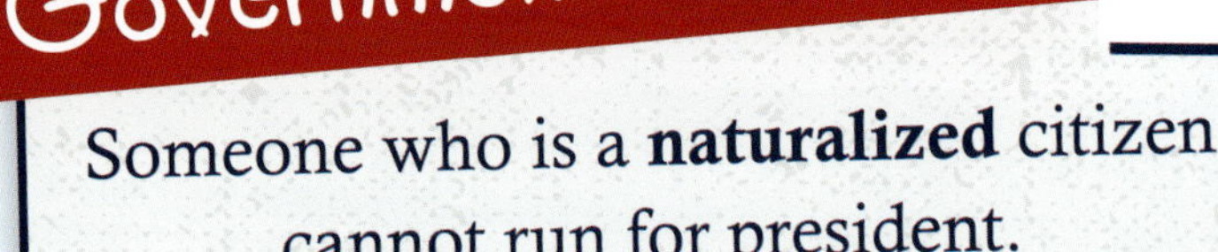

Government Guides

Someone who is a **naturalized** citizen cannot run for president.

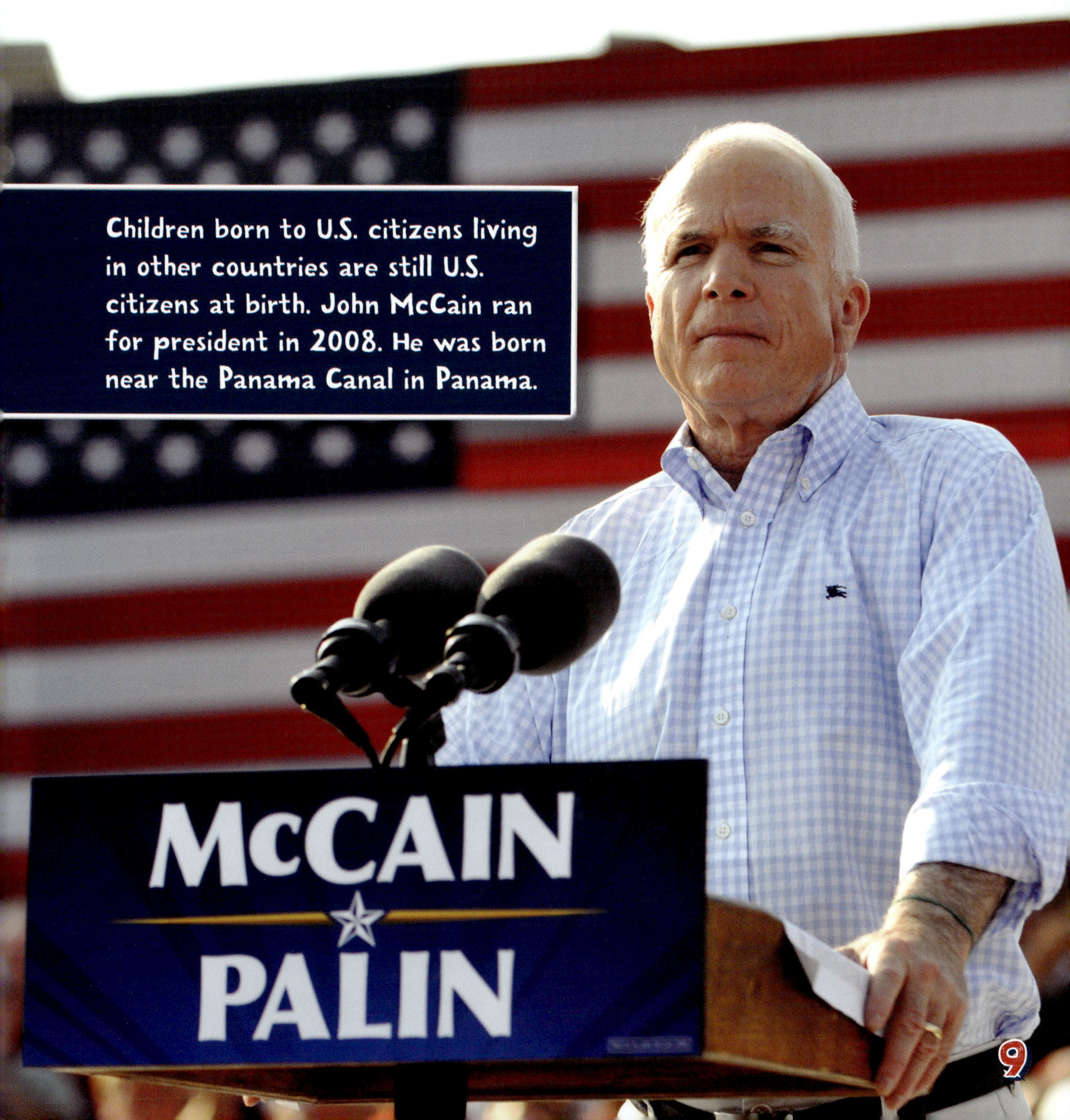

Children born to U.S. citizens living in other countries are still U.S. citizens at birth. John McCain ran for president in 2008. He was born near the Panama Canal in Panama.

Two-Party System

Candidates are those who are running for president. They must meet the three requirements for a president as written in the Constitution. But that's the only guidance the Constitution gives!

Someone running for president can be a man or a woman. They can be of any race or faith. They can have any political beliefs.

However, only men have been U.S. president. All but one of them has been white. Today, it is most likely that someone from the two largest **political parties**—the Democratic Party or Republican Party—will be elected.

Hillary Clinton was the first woman to become a major political party's presidential candidate in 2016. She ran as part of the Democratic Party.

Before They Were President

Ronald Reagan was an actor before he was U.S. president. Ulysses S. Grant and Dwight D. Eisenhower were generals in the U.S. armed forces. Harry S. Truman owned a clothing store. Donald Trump was a businessman. They show that a U.S. president can come from any **professional** background!

Still, most U.S. presidents have been lawyers or held government office. Many presidents have done both! Thomas Jefferson worked as a lawyer before holding posts in Virginia's government, including governor.

When Ronald Reagan was young, he was a lifeguard! All kinds of life experiences can lead to the White House.

Government Guides

President Gerald Ford worked at Yellowstone National Park as a young man before he was president. He said working there was "one of the greatest summers of my life."

Not Allowed

There are two Constitutional amendments, or additions, that say who *cannot* be president. The 14th Amendment says any government official who has been part of **insurrection** or **rebellion** cannot be a member of Congress, president, or vice president. This is called the disqualification clause. It was written to keep leaders of the **Confederacy** out of power.

The 22nd Amendment states that a person can only serve two terms as president. So, anyone who was already elected president twice cannot run for president again!

Many argue Donald Trump caused an insurrection after a crowd of his supporters attacked the Capitol Building on January 6, 2021. However, this didn't stop Trump from being elected president again in 2024.

Government Guides

Disqualification means taking away a right or power. The disqualification clause hasn't been used much in the present day. Politicians disagree about how it might be used.

Time to Nominate

To run for president, a candidate needs to be on the ballot! Most of the time, this means they need to earn a major party's nomination.

First, states hold either a primary or a caucus where party members vote for a candidate. In most states, the person who gets the most votes earns all of a state's delegates. Delegates then vote for that candidate at their political party's convention. The person who earns the most delegates gets the party's nomination.

Let's Talk About Elections!

ballot
A sheet of paper listing candidates' names and used for voting.

caucus
A closed meeting of people from the same political party used to select a presidential nominee.

convention
A gathering of people who have a common interest or purpose.

delegate
Person chosen to represent, or stand for, their state at a political party's convention to choose a presidential nominee.

nomination
The act of being nominated, or proposed as a candidate for election to office.

primary
An election in which members of the same political party run against one another for the opportunity to run in a major election.

To understand how someone can run for president, you have to understand how U.S. elections work. Here are some of the words you need to know!

Third-Party Candidates

A candidate can run for president as the nominee for a smaller political party, often called a third party. A candidate may run as an independent, or someone not part of any political party.

How a third-party or independent presidential candidate gets on the ballot depends on the state. In some states, certain third parties got enough votes in past years' elections to earn a spot. Other states make candidates turn in a petition, which is a paper thousands of people living in the state have signed.

Jill Stein

Government Guides

In 2024, Green Party candidate Jill Stein talked about the part third-party candidates play in the presidential election: "Our role here is to bring up these **issues** that are not going to get raised by politics as usual."

Although it's often harder for third-party candidates to run for president, they can still make waves. Ralph Nader, who ran for the Green Party in 2008, is an example!

The Finish Line

Running for president is hard work! All presidential candidates travel across the country meeting voters. They give speeches telling the American people what they would do if elected. It costs a lot of money to do this. Candidates spend millions of dollars to try and reach voters.

Then, the candidates face off in a general election. As the Constitution says, presidential elections are held every four years on the first Tuesday after the first Monday in November.

Think About It!

Anyone who meets the Constitutional requirements for president can run—but it's hard if you aren't part of one of the two main political parties. Do you think this is good for the country? Why or why not?

General elections are those any U.S. citizens over age 18 can vote in. The person who wins the most **electoral votes** wins the presidency!

Glossary

Confederacy: The Confederate States of America, or the group of states that left the United States during the American Civil War.

elect: To choose for a position in a government.

electoral vote: A vote from a process called the Electoral College in which electors are chosen and cast votes that represent each state's votes for president and vice president.

experience: Skills gained by doing something.

insurrection: The act of trying to overthrow or stop a government from working.

issue: A matter two sides disagree about.

naturalized: Having to do with someone born in a different country becoming a citizen.

politics: The activities of the government and government officials.

political party: A group of people with similar beliefs about how a government should be run.

professional: Having to do with a job someone does for a living.

rebellion: A fight to overthrow a government.

Supreme Court: The highest court in the United States.

For More Information

Books

Finn, Peter. *Electing the President.* Buffalo, NY: Cavendish Square Publishing, 2025.

Morrison, Marie. *20 Things You Didn't Know About the Presidency.* Buffalo, NY: PowerKids Press, 2025.

Winn, Kevin P. What *Does the Vice President Do?* Ann Arbor, MI: Cherry Lake Press, 2023.

Websites

The Three Branches of the U.S. Government
https://kids.nationalgeographic.com/history/article/three-branches-of-government
Find out more about the part the executive branch plays in the U.S. government.

The Electoral Collage
https://www.ducksters.com/history/us_government/electoral_college.php
Learn more about the process of electing the U.S. president here.

What Is a Political Party?
https://ny.pbslearningmedia.org/resource/what-is-a-political-party-video/wviz-politics-on-point/
Watch a video about what political parties are here.

Publisher's note to educators and parents: Our editors have carefully reviewed these websites to ensure that they are suitable for students. Many websites change frequently, however, and we cannot guarantee that a site's future contents will continue to meet our high standards of quality and educational value. Be advised that students should be closely supervised whenever they access the internet.

Index